MW01290112

39 ESL Warm-Ups:

For Kids (7+)

Jackie Bolen

Jennifer Booker Smith

Edited by Tristan K. Hicks

All rights reserved. No part of this publication may be reproduced, distributed, or transmitted in any form or by any means, including photocopying, recording or other electronic or mechanical means without the prior written permission of the publisher, except in the case of brief quotations in critical reviews and certain other non-commercial uses permitted by copyright law. For permission requests, write to the publisher/author at the address below.

Jackie Bolen: wealthyenglishteacher@gmail.com

Jennifer Booker Smith: jenniferteacher@gmail.com

Table of Contents

About the Author: Jackie Bolen

I've been teaching English in South Korea for a decade to every level and type of student, including everyone from kindergarten kids to adults. Most of my time has been centered on teaching at two universities: five years at a science and engineering school out in the rice paddies of Chungcheongnam-Do, and also at a major university in Busan where I now teach high level classes for English major students. In my spare time, you can usually find me outside surfing, biking, hiking or on the hunt for the most delicious kimchi I can find.

In case you were wondering, I hold a Master of Arts in Psychology. During my time in Korea I've successfully completed both the Cambridge CELTA and DELTA certification programs. With the combination of almost ten years teaching ESL/EFL and my more formal teaching qualifications, I have a solid foundation to offer teaching advice. I truly hope that you find this book useful and would love it if you sent me an email with any questions or feedback that you might have—I'll always take the time to personally respond (wealthyenglishteacher@gmail.com).

More Fabulous Stuff to Check Out

If you find this book useful, please leave a review over on Amazon and don't forget to check out my other books at the same time:

The Wealthy English Teacher is a book in which you can learn all about finances for ESL teachers. You could also check out the book's website at www.wealthyenglishteacher.com. If you're interested in getting the most awesome job in South Korea which is working at a university—please check out *How to Get a University Job in South Korea*. You can find more details at the book's website www.universityjobskorea.com.

If you teach speaking or conversation classes check out *39 No-Prep/Low-Prep ESL Speaking Activities: For Teenagers and Adults.* Or, the version for children that Jennifer and I wrote together: 39 No-Prep/Low-Prep ESL Speaking Activities for Kids.

Jackie Bolen around the Internet

ESL Speaking (www.eslspeaking.org)

Twitter (@bolen_jackie)

About the Author: Jennifer Booker Smith

I have a Master of Education degree in TESOL and have spent fifteen years teaching students of all ages in Korea, from two-year-old preschoolers to businessmen. I've even been a teacher trainer at a university of education. However, my greatest loves are the middle primary grades—I left a fairly cushy teacher trainer position to return to the elementary classroom. In that age group, I've taught all ability levels from false beginner to near-native returnees.

During my time in the classroom, I've created countless board and card games and other resources. In this book, you'll find some of the activities which I have used successfully (I've tried plenty which weren't successful!) in a variety of settings; these are the ones I've used again and again because they actually work.

When I'm not teaching, like Jackie, you can often find me hiking. I've recently taken up running, and will soon be running my second half marathon. While teaching takes up more "free" time than non-teachers realize, it's important to recharge the batteries. Being outside is my favorite way to do just that.

You can get in touch with me by emailing jenniferteacher@gmail.com. I'd love to hear from you and help you with your classes in any way that I can, particularly if you have a difficult children's class and would like some advice. I'll do my best to assist you.

About the Editor: Tristan K. Hicks

My areas of expertise are teaching, study abroad, editing and budget travel. I grew up in a family of educators, so I've been teaching in one form or another since the age of fifteen. During the course of my education I studied full-time in six countries, picking up a TEFL certification, a bachelor's and two master's degrees along the way.

I've edited dozens and dozens of academic papers, theses, articles and CVs. My specialization is editing for content and style for non-native speakers of English. If you're looking for help with proofing or editing, contact me at Tristan.Hicks@gmail.com

I am also a study abroad and travel correspondent for VagabondJourney.com. You can find some of my articles at my author page here.

Why Use Warm-Ups?

Warm-ups are short activities used at the beginning of class. Many feel that they are a waste of time but they are definitely not! Many of your students will not have spoken English or given the language a single thought since you last saw them. By beginning your lesson with a warm-up activity, you are easing them back into using English and orienting them to be more focused on the lesson ahead.

With just a bit of planning, your warm-up can review a previous lesson or recycle older material to refresh your students' memories. You can also preview a new topic and begin class with a clearer idea of their familiarity with the material. Based on their performance with the warm-up, you can mentally adjust your lesson, if necessary, rather than change track once you have gotten started.

In this way, warm-ups aren't just good for your students, they are good for you as an informal assessment tool. How well have they retained that lesson you are reviewing? Are there any apparent gaps in their understanding? Does that student who received 100% on last week's quiz seem to have forgotten everything? Tests only tell part of the story, so take advantage of informal assessment opportunities whenever possible.

Warm-Ups for All Levels

Make a Sentence

Skill: Writing

Age: All

Materials Required: None, or worksheet/white board/PowerPoint

To practice current or review vocabulary, have students make 1-5 sentences.

No materials version: Have students use their books and choose a given number of words to make sentences.

White board/PowerPoint version: Give students a list of words to use all or some of.

Worksheet/PowerPoint version: Fill-in-the-blank or multiple choice with a word bank.

Procedure:

Begin with a brief oral review of the vocabulary words you want them to work with, eliciting from the students what the words mean.

No prep version: Have students take out their books and notebooks and tell them a number of sentences to make using those words. For example, "Turn to page 53, and choose three vocabulary words. In your notebook, write a new sentence using each word."

White board/PowerPoint version: Either give students a word list to choose from, or for lower level classes, several sentences with a word bank. Have the class write the complete sentences in their notebooks.

One Question Review

Skills: Speaking/writing

Age: All

Materials Required: None, optional: White board

Ask one question about the previous lesson to spark students' recall. This is very useful for gauging students' recall and understanding, particularly when continuing with a unit. For a very quick warm-up, choose a volunteer to answer the question and check several other students for comprehension of the answer. Otherwise, have students write a brief answer of 1-3 sentences. These are a good quick informal assessment or could be used as a pop quiz.

Procedure:

1. Begin by eliciting from students what they remember from the previous class.

2. Once they have given a few answers, ask them one question. This could either direct them to some aspect of the lesson which they have not mentioned (for example, the main idea of a story) or it could dig a little deeper, more like a follow up question.

3. Have students write their answer in 1-3 sentences in their notebook.

Question of the Day

Skills: Speaking/writing

Age: All

Materials Required: None

Ask a question to spark a short student discussion. Current events, new movies, etc. are good topics to get kids speaking in English for a few minutes at the beginning of class. If there is a new blockbuster out, that will be of interest to most students. The ones who have seen it can briefly summarize and answer the other students' questions about it.

Procedure:

1. Begin class by asking students how they have been and if anything interesting has been happening lately.

2. Use one of the students' answers as a segue to a current events question, such as, "You saw _____ last weekend? Who else saw that? What happened?" Just pick a movie, sporting event, or other topic that the majority of students are likely to have seen or at least know.

Picture Prompt

Skills: Speaking/listening

Age: All

Materials: Picture/PowerPoint image

Show students an image and have them generate questions or speculate about the picture. For lower level students, this can be purely descriptive:

Q: What do you see?

A: I see a house, a car, and some people.

Q: What color is the car?

A: It is blue.

For high beginner/low intermediate students, have an image which can generate questions such as:

What is happening in this picture?

How does that person feel?

Why do you think so?

For more advanced students, have an unusual image. Encourage them to create a narrative to explain the story. This activity can also be done as a Quick Write.

Teaching Tips:

You can find collections of unusual images online which are perfect for advanced students to create their narratives. If you want to use this as a writing activity with beginner or low intermediate students, give them a worksheet of questions to answer.

Procedure:

1. In advance, prepare an image, either PowerPoint or a picture large enough for the class to easily see.

2. Divide students into pairs or small groups.

3. Depending on the level of the students:

Elicit descriptive sentences about the image. Encourage them to make their own questions to ask a partner.

Have them discuss what they think is happening in the picture, how the person/ people feel and why they think so, etc.

Have them create a narrative about the image. (Unusual images work well for this.)

4. Optionally, have them write their responses.

Word of the Day

Skills: Writing

Age: All

Materials Required: White board/PowerPoint

I have frequently been required to either give my students a word, quote, or idiom of the day, outside of our usual text, but usually related to the text or a monthly theme. You can easily start a Word of the Day activity for your students, by giving them a single word each day from their text (but not a vocabulary word), current events, or have a theme for each month.

Write the word on the white board or PowerPoint along with the definition, part of speech, and several example sentences. Have students copy all of this in their notebook in a section for their Words of the Day. You can use the word as an exit ticket, have a weekly quiz, or add one or two words to each regular vocabulary quiz.

Variation (more advanced): Idiom of the Day where you give students an idiom with a definition and a picture (if possible). Have them make 1-3 sentences using it correctly.

Procedure:

1. In advance, prepare a collection of words from your students' textbook, but not part of the vocabulary list.
2. Begin each day (or one day per week) with one new word. Introduce the word, just as you would their regular vocabulary: present the word, the definition, part of speech, and several example sentences.
3. Have students copy the sentences in the notebooks and add their own sentence.
4. Add all or some Words of the Day to your regular vocabulary quizzes.

Q & A

Skills: Writing

Age: All

Materials Required: None, or worksheet/white board/PowerPoint

In this activity, students will use one vocabulary word to make a question and another to answer the question.

No materials version: Students will use their vocabulary list/text book to choose their two words.

Worksheet/white board/PowerPoint version: Give your students a word list to work from. This is good if you want to review specific terms, or if you want students to focus on specific terms from their current vocabulary list.

Procedure:

1. In advance, prepare a worksheet or PowerPoint with a word bank of vocabulary words. Otherwise, write a word list on the white board or tell your students which page in their text book you want them to work from.

2. Have students write two sentences in their notebooks: one should ask a question using a vocabulary word and the other should answer the question using a different vocabulary word.

3. Give students a time limit of 3-5 minutes.

Word-Definition Match

Skills: Reading

Age: All

Materials Required: Cards or worksheet/white board/PowerPoint

Card version: Print one word or definition per card. You will need one set per student, pair or group. (This version is good for pair/small group work and adds a speaking component to the task.)

Worksheet/white board/PowerPoint version: Create a word bank of current or review vocabulary and a list of definitions for students to draw a line (worksheet) or match letters and numbers for white board or PowerPoint.

Procedure (Card version):

1. In advance, prepare cards with one word or definition per card. Print and laminate enough

for each student, pair, or group to have a set.

2. If having students work in pairs or small groups, divide the class accordingly and distribute a full set of cards to each. If students will be working alone, give each student a set of cards.

3. Have students match the words to their definitions as quickly as possible.

Procedure (Worksheet/white board/PowerPoint version):

1. Have students match the words and definitions, by drawing a line (worksheet) or match letters and numbers, writing their answers in their notebooks.

2. Have students trade papers to check.

Sentence Type Review

Skills: Writing

Age: 8+

Materials Required: Worksheets/white board/PowerPoint

This is a good way to quickly check your students' understanding/recollection of sentence types. Create a short worksheet using the different types of sentences (declarative, interrogative, exclamatory, imperative or simple, compound, complex). For beginners, have them simply identify what type of sentence it is. You may even have an example of each sentence type, rather than an answer bank.

For more advanced students, have them change the sentences from one type to another. For example, change an interrogative to a declarative, or change a complex sentence into two simple sentences. Or have them use that week's vocabulary and write one simple, one compound, and one complex sentence. Remember to keep it short, so it can be completed in about five minutes. Here's an example of this activity: www.eslspeaking.org/sentence-type-review.

Procedure:

1. In advance, prepare a worksheet or PowerPoint, or write several sentences on the white board.

2. Begin class with a brief review of the sentence types your activity will cover.

3. According to the level of the class, have students either identify the type of sentence (lower level) or change the sentences from one type to another (higher level).

4. Have students write their answers in their notebooks, if working from the white board or PowerPoint.

Categories

Skills: Speaking/listening/writing

Age: All

Materials Required: None, optional: butcher paper/A3 paper

Students can review by brainstorming words they know in a given category, such as food, job, hobbies, etc.

Variation 1: Students work in small groups, making a list of all the words they can think of for that category. The group with the longest list wins.

Variation 2: Students take turns adding one word at a time to the list. If a student repeats a word or says a word which doesn't fit, they are out. This variation is better suited to small classes or groups working independently.

Procedure:

1. Begin by dividing students into groups of 3-5. Small classes can work as a whole.

2. Give each group a piece of A3 or butcher paper. (For a speaking/listening activity, have

students take turns adding a word. If students can't add a word, they are out.)

3. Give the class a category, such as jobs or animals and a time limit (about 3 minutes) to brainstorm and write as many words that match the category as possible.

4. The group with the most correct words wins.

I'm Going on a Picnic

Skills: Listening/speaking

Age: 8+

Materials Required: None

This is an oldie, but a goodie. It gets students talking and thinking critically. Think of a rule for items on the picnic, but don't tell the class. For example, "must contain the letter E," or, "must be countable." Tell them you are going on a picnic, and give examples of 3-5 items you are taking with you, to give them hints about your rule. Then, elicit from the students what they would take. If their item doesn't fit your rule, tell them they can't take it.

To keep wait times between turns shorter, have large classes work in groups of 2-3 , rather than individually. In any case, set a time limit for each person or group making a guess (30-60 seconds, according to their level), or they are out. The group to guess the rule wins.

Note: groups are not out if they suggest an item that doesn't match the rule, or if they guess the wrong rule. The time limit is to keep the game moving, and disqualifying students for not making guesses keeps students from just listening to other guesses to guess the rule without contributing otherwise.

Procedure:

1. Think of a rule for items which can go on the picnic, such as "must contain the letter E," or,

"must be countable."

2. Tell the class you are going on a picnic, and give examples of 3-5 items you are taking with you, to give them hints about your rule.

3. Elicit from the students what they would take. If their item doesn't fit your rule, tell them they can't take it.

4. Have large classes work in groups of 2-3, and set a 30-60 second time limit to keep wait times between turns shorter.

5. The group to guess the rule wins.

Vocabulary Word Hunt

Skills: Reading/writing

Age: 7+

Materials Required: Worksheet

Make a 3 x 3 grid with clues about 9 vocabulary words and include a word bank. Have students use their dictionaries or glossaries to race to get 1/2/3 Bingos or complete the grid. Here's an example of vocabulary word hunt: www.eslspeaking.org/vocabularyulary-word-hunt.

Procedure:

1. In advance, prepare 3 x 3 grids filled with clues about 9 vocabulary words and a word bank.

2. Have students use their dictionaries or glossaries to get 1/2/3 Bingos or complete the grid.

3. The first student to correctly match the words with the definitions wins.

"What Can I do with a _____?"

Skills: Speaking/listening

Age: All

Materials Required: An object

Show students some random common object (potatoes are often used for this activity, but I

17

like to use some kind of "trash" to introduce a lesson on recycling.) Have students work as a class or in small groups to brainstorm as many possible uses for the item as possible. Give them a time limit (3-5 minutes), then discuss their answers. If some answers seem too outlandish, have the student or group explain how or why they would use the item in that way.

Procedure:

1. In advance, prepare an object. A potato is commonly used, but it can be anything.

2. Divide students into groups of 3-5.

3. Give them 3-5 minutes to brainstorm creative uses for the object.

4. As a class, briefly discuss their various ideas.

5. You can have the class choose the best idea, if you like.

Mystery Box

Skills: Speaking

Age: All

Materials Required: Several small objects, a box

I like to use this activity just after studying adjectives. I'll make sure we have learned words that describe texture as well as the usual size and shape words. This is a fun activity, but it is best with small classes due to the time it takes for each student to have a turn.

Before class, you will need to prepare a large shoe box or similar, by cutting a hole slightly larger than fist-sized and covering the hole. You can use garland or tissue paper, but a handkerchief is fastest and easiest. Whatever you use, the students should not be able to see inside the box, but they should be able to stick their hand inside.

One by one, have students take turns feeling inside the box. As they feel, ask them questions about the size, shape, texture, etc. Once everyone has had a turn, review the answers students gave while feeling and elicit guesses as to what is in the box. As students guess items correctly, pull them from the box. If no one can guess some items, end by showing them to the class.

Due to the time involved with each child feeling inside the box, this activity is best suited to small classes. You can use anything (not sharp), but children's toys are good for this, as well as letter magnets.

Procedure:

1. In advance, prepare a large shoe box or copy paper box by cutting a hand-sized hole and then covering it with a handkerchief, so students can reach in but can't see inside.

2. Place several small (not sharp!) objects inside. The class should know the names of the objects.

3. Have students take turns reaching in the box and feeling the objects.

4. As students feel the objects, ask them questions about the size, shape, and texture of the items.

5. When everyone has had a turn, elicit guesses from the students about what they think the objects are.

6. As students correctly identify items, remove them from the box. If the class cannot guess some items, end the activity by showing the remaining items to the class.

Match Pictures and Sentences

Skills: Reading/speaking/listening

Age: All

Materials Required: Picture cards and sentence cards

This activity has a bit more prep, so try to save it for something you can use in multiple ways. Divide class into groups of 2-4, and give each group a complete set of sentence cards and picture cards. The students should match a sentence to a picture, racing to be the first group to correctly match all cards.

For lower level students, the items should be quite clearly different, but higher level students can have more ambiguous choices, so they have to consider more carefully the best matches. Depending on the level of the students and the time available, give each group 5-10 sentences and corresponding pictures.

Teaching Tips:

This is a good leveled activity for mixed-ability classes. Divide students into groups of similar ability levels, and give each group level-appropriate sentences.

For an added challenge, have the sentences tell a story, which students must correctly order after matching the cards.

This can be easily adapted to a jigsaw activity by giving each student only 1 or 2 cards and having them mingle to find the match.

Procedure:

1. In advance, prepare a set of 5-10 picture cards and sentence cards which describe the pictures.

2. Divide students into groups of 2-4 and give each group a complete set of cards.

3. Have groups correctly match the pairs of cards as quickly as possible.

Words in Words

Skills: Writing

Age: 8+

Materials Required: Worksheet/white board/PowerPoint

You probably did this when you were in school. Give students a word and have them make as many words as possible using the letters in that word. For example, vacation: a, on, no, act, action, taco, ant, van… You can give a point for each word, so the student with the most words wins, or give more points for longer words. When time is up (about 5 minutes), show students the possible answers.

Wordles.com has a tool which allows you to type in a word and get the possible words. For vacation, they listed 45 words, some of which I should have thought of myself and some of which are "Scrabble words". Since your students will not possibly know all of these words, so it is up to you whether you show all answers or an abridged list.

Procedure:

1. In advance, prepare a long word and write it on the white board or a PowerPoint or give students individual worksheets.

2. Give students a time limit of about 5 minutes to make words from the letters in the word.

3. To make it a competition, when time is up, you can give students points for each word.

4. When the activity is finished, show students all of the possible words they could have made. You can get these from www.wordles.com.

Word Poem / Name Poem

Skills: Writing

Age: 8+

Materials Required: Example poem poster/PowerPoint

Another activity you undoubtedly did yourself as a student. Either give students a word related to the lesson, or have them use their names (a great ice breaker activity, too!) They simply begin each line with a letter from the word, so that the first letter of each line read vertically spells the word. Using that letter, write a word or phrase that describes the word.

Here's an example word poem: www.eslspeaking.org/word-poem.

Teaching Tip:

These are great for decorating the classroom or including in student portfolios. So, have them make a final draft on copy paper and decorate. The final draft can be done as homework.

Procedure:

1. In advance, prepare your own name or word poem to display for students.

2. Show them that the first letter of each line spells a word.

3. Give them a word related to your lesson or have them use their names to make their own poem.

Odd One Out

Skills: Speaking

Age: All

Materials Required: None, or white board/PowerPoint, optional: "One of These Things" song (on YouTube).

Here is another activity to promote critical thinking. Just like the Sesame Street game, give students four items which seem similar, but one which doesn't belong. Have students work in groups to decide what doesn't belong and why. For example, bat, bird, lizard, frog. Answer: bats, because they don't lay eggs, or birds, because they have feathers.

Teaching Tips:

For more advanced students, you can simply tell them the four items, but for lower level students, you should have the four items written on the white board or PowerPoint, or show four images on a PowerPoint for them to refer to.

Procedure:

1. Optional: begin by showing the Sesame Street song "One of the These Things." Stop the video before the answer and elicit guesses from the students.

2. Give students four items which seem similar, but one doesn't belong. For example, bat, bird, lizard, frog. Answer: bats, because they don't lay eggs, or birds, because they have feathers.

3. Give students 3 minutes to decide in groups of 2-4 which doesn't belong and why.

4. As a class, discuss their answers.

Quick Read

Skills: Reading/writing/speaking

Age: All

Materials Required: Worksheet

Give students a short passage, slightly below their level, and 3-5 comprehension questions. It should be short enough to be completed in 7-8 minutes.

This is a good way to recycle previous material by summarizing a story or part of a story. You can also use this as a pre-test before beginning a new lesson to gauge their existing knowledge of a topic or the relevant vocabulary

Procedure:

1. In advance, prepare a short passage using language slightly below the level of the class.

2. Include 3-5 comprehension questions and an example question demonstrating how to answer.

3. Give students 7-8 minutes to read and answer the questions.

Memory Tray

Skills: Speaking

Age: 8+

Materials Required: A tray with several items/PowerPoint/white board and flashcards

Before class, prepare a tray with 10-20 items, depending on the age of the students. Keep it covered while you tell the students they will have a short time to study the tray. Give 20 seconds to a minute, depending on their age and the number of items. If the class is large, a PowerPoint with images, or flashcards on the white board may be better if you can cover and uncover your white board.

When everyone is ready, uncover the items for the allotted time, then re-cover them. Have students work in pairs or small groups to reconstruct the tray.

Variation 1: Students simply need to list the items they saw.

Variation 2: Students need to recall the location of the items in relation to one another.

Teaching Tip:

If you have them come look more closely, remind them to look but not touch, or some competitive students may pocket some items.

Procedure:

1. In advance, prepare a tray of 10-20 items (more for older students) or a PowerPoint with images or flashcards to put on the white board.

2. Divide the class into pairs or small groups and tell them to look carefully at the items.

3. Tell students not to write anything down.

4. Reveal the items for 20-60 seconds, depending on how many items there are.

5. Have the students work with their partners for 2-3 minutes to reconstruct what they saw.

6. The group with the most correct items wins.

Just a Minute

Skills: Speaking

Age: 9+

Materials Required: White board, timer

This is a very simple activity that you can use as a fast warm-up at the beginning of class in order to get your students talking. Write a bunch of general categories on the board such as jobs, hobbies, dreams, movies, food, etc. Put the students into groups of 4 and they can number themselves 1-2-3-4. Then, ask one of the students to throw a paper airplane at the board and whatever word it gets closest to is the topic for the first student. All the number ones must talk about that topic for one minute without stopping and if they stop or have a long pause, they've lost the challenge. You can adjust the time limit to be higher or lower depending on the level of students (beginner = 30 seconds, advanced = 2 minutes). Erase the first speaking round word from the board and continue the activity with the remaining three students except that they have different topics. It's helpful if the teacher does an example speech first with a topic that the students choose.

Teaching Tip:

For higher level students, you can require that their teammates listen carefully and each of them has to ask the speaker an *interesting* follow-up question.

Procedure:

1. The teacher writes topics on the white board (teacher-supplied, or elicited from students).

2. Put students into groups of 4. They number themselves 1-2-3-4.

3. The teacher does an example speech with a topic that students choose.

4. One student throws a paper airplane at the white board. The topic closest to where it hits is the first one.

5. Student one has to talk about that topic for a minute without stopping. The goal is to have minimal pauses and to never stop talking. (Optional: the other three students each ask a follow-up question).

6. Erase the first speaking round word. Another student throws the paper airplane and finds another topic. The number two students talk for a minute. Continue with the third and fourth rounds' students.

Warm-Ups for Lower-Level Students

Part of Speech Review

Skills: Writing

Age: All

Materials Required: Worksheet/white board/PowerPoint

Give the students several sentences and have them do one of the following: identify the part of speech of underlined words; circle (nouns/verbs/adjectives...); or add a word of the correct part of speech (fill in or multiple choice). Scaffold with an example of the activity done correctly as well as examples of the part of speech being focused on, such as a list of 5-6 nouns they know.

For an example of this activity, using possessive pronouns, check out: www.eslspeaking.org/part-of-speech.

Procedure:

1. In advance, prepare several sentences either on a worksheet or PowerPoint, or write them on the white board.

2. Give students at least one example demonstrating how you would like the activity to be completed, for example, fill in the blank or circle the noun.

3. Begin the activity by eliciting from the students several examples of the given part of speech. Add to the list if necessary.

4. Give the students 2-5 minutes to complete the activity, depending on whether they need to write the sentences in their notebook or complete a worksheet.

5. Have students exchange papers and check answers.

Word Choice

Skills: Writing

Age: All

Materials Required: Worksheet/white board/PowerPoint

This can be used to review subject/object pronouns, adjectives/adverbs, etc. by having students choose the correct word. Give the students several sentences with a blank and two possible answers. Students should write the sentences correctly. To make the activity easier, students can simply circle the correct word. To make the activity more challenging, have students fill in the blanks, with or without a word bank.

Procedure:

1. In advance, prepare several sentences either on a worksheet or PowerPoint, or write them on the white board.

2. Give students at least one example demonstrating how you would like the activity to be completed, for example, fill in the blank with the adjective.

3. Begin the activity by eliciting from the students several examples of the two choices they have, such as subject and object pronouns, and when to use them. Add to the list, if necessary.

4. Give the students 2-5 minutes to complete the activity, depending on whether they need to write the sentences in their notebook or complete a worksheet.

5. Have students exchange papers and check answers.

Sentence Word Order

Skills: Writing

Age: All

Materials Required: Sentence cards, worksheet/white board/PowerPoint

Students whose first languages have different subject/verb/object order than English need practice with the correct grammatical structures. Give students several sentences with some words in the wrong order. Have students rewrite the sentences correctly. Here's an example of the sentence word order activity: www.eslspeaking.org/sentence-word-order.

Sentence card version: you will need to have one card with several sentences or several cards with one sentence each per student/pair/small group. This version is better for having students work together, adding a speaking component to the activity, or as an early finisher activity.

Worksheet version: Give students space to correctly write the sentences or choose the correct of two options.

White board/PowerPoint version: Give students several sentences for them to write correctly in their notebooks.

Teaching Tip:

Sentence cards are simply cards with sentences. This creates a bit of a wild card element, since everyone gets something different and is good for classes with students who tend to copy one another or for using as an early finisher activity. Don't forget to laminate them and begin with an example.

Procedure:

1. In advance, prepare several sentences either on sentence cards, a worksheet or PowerPoint, or write them on the white board.

2. Give students at least one example demonstrating how you would like the activity to be completed, showing a mixed up sentence with the correction.

3. Begin the activity by completing several examples of the activity as a class.

4. Give the students 2-5 minutes to complete the activity, depending on whether they need to write the sentences in their notebook or complete a worksheet.

5. Have students exchange papers and check answers.

Punctuation/Capitalization

Skills: Writing

Age: All

Materials Required: Worksheet/white board/PowerPoint

Younger students and those whose first languages have different punctuation and/or capitalization rules than English need frequent practice in order to master correct usage. Have students correct several sentences, adding punctuation and capital letters as needed. For lower level and younger students, focus on one element at a time, such as the word "I" or using commas in a list. More advanced students can have a mix, but since this is a short activity, keep it to one correction per sentence. As with the Word Choice activity, students should write the sentences correctly. To make the activity easier, students can simply circle the correct word. To make the activity more challenging, have students fill in the blanks, with or without a word bank.

Procedure:

1. In advance, prepare several sentences either on a worksheet or PowerPoint, or write them

on the white board.

2. Give students at least one example demonstrating how you would like the activity to be completed, for example, add commas to a list.

3. Begin the activity by completing several examples of the activity as a class.

4. Give the students 2-5 minutes to complete the activity, depending on whether they need to write the sentences in their notebook or complete a worksheet.

5. Have students exchange papers and check answers.

ABC Order

Skills: Writing

Age: All

Materials Required: Worksheet/white board/PowerPoint

Young students and those whose first languages do not use the Latin alphabet need to practice alphabetic order. Have students order their vocabulary or another word list alphabetically. For lowest level beginners, have no more than one word starting with any given letter.

Procedure:

1. In advance, prepare several vocabulary words either on a worksheet or PowerPoint, or write them on the white board.

2. With young students, begin with the Alphabet Song.

3. Then, have the class work together to help you put several words in alphabetical order.

4. Give the students 2-5 minutes to complete the activity, depending on the number of words and the students' level.

5. Have students exchange papers and check answers.

Subject-Predicate Practice

Skills: Writing

Age: All

Materials Required: Worksheet/white board/PowerPoint

This is a quick grammar practice activity. Depending on the level of the class, have them simply identify subjects and predicates, complete sentences by adding one or the other, or have students add details to the subject or predicate (adjective/adverb practice).

Procedure:

1. In advance, prepare several sentences on a worksheet or PowerPoint or write them on the white board.

2. Give students at least one example demonstrating how you would like the activity to be completed, for example, circle the subject or complete the sentence by adding a subject.

3. Begin the activity by completing several examples of the activity as a class.

4. Give the students 3-5 minutes to complete the activity, depending on whether they need to write the sentences in their notebook or complete a worksheet.

5. Have students exchange papers and check answers. If they are creating their own subjects or predicates, you may want to collect them to check yourself.

Warm-Ups for Higher-Level Students

Talking Bag

Skills: Speaking/listening

Age: 8+

Materials Required: Questions cards, bag/box/bowl

Procedure:

In advance, prepare a bag (or box, bowl, etc) full of question cards (laminate them!)

Variation 1: Draw a question from the bag and read/ write it. Have students ask and answer the question with the person next to them.

Variation 2: Choose one student to draw a question. That student asks the question to one student, who then draws a question to ask a third student. Before beginning, set a time limit or decide how many students will have a turn.

Variation 3: Divide students into small groups of 3-5. Have one member of each group draw one question to ask, and have each group member take turns answering.

OR

Have each student draw one question to ask their group.

Top That (Four Yorkshiremen)

Skills: Speaking/listening

Age: 10+

Materials Required: Four Yorkshiremen sketch (subtitled version)

Show the Monty Python "Four Yorkshiremen" sketch to introduce the concept of one-upmanship. Ask some comprehension checking questions before telling the class a mundane story to get them started. Invite a student to top your story. Then, in small groups, have each group member take a turn topping the previous student's story.

Procedure:

1. Show the Monty Python "Four Yorkshiremen" sketch and follow up with a few comprehension checking questions to make sure they understand the concept of one-upmanship.

2. Tell them a fairly mundane story to get them started and invite a student to top your story.

3. Divide the class into groups of 3-5 and have them take turns topping the previous student's stories.

Five-Minute Debate

Skills: Speaking/listening

Age: 10+

Materials Required: None

Give students an age-appropriate controversial statement. If you are knowledgeable about pop culture, you can start with, "so and so is the best X (singer, soccer player, whatever)," if your students are too young for truly controversial topics. In pairs or small groups, have them debate the sides. You may have to assign sides, if too many agree or disagree with your premise.

You may need to scaffold with language like, "I think _____, because _____." "I agree with X, but _____."

Teaching Tips:

If your students need some scaffolding with language, it would be helpful for them to have it written on the white board or a PowerPoint.

Procedure:

1. Divide students into pairs or small groups.

2. Give students a controversial statement. I would prepare this in advance, focusing on a recent news item or pop culture, but you could probably think of something on the fly if you needed something on the spot.

3. Give students a time limit to discuss the merits of their side, trying to change the mind of their "opponent".

4. If necessary, begin with some helpful language, such as, "I feel ___, because ___."

5. Finish with a quick poll to see if anyone changed their side.

Reported Speech

Skills: Writing/reading/speaking

Age: 8+

Materials: None, or sentence cards, or worksheet/white board/PowerPoint

Reported speech can be difficult for students, so a little regular practice can help make it more automatic.

No materials version: Ask student A a question. Ask student B to "report" student A's answer. Model the activity first by simply asking a student a question and then reporting the answer to the class. Example:

T: What day is it today?

A: Today is Tuesday.

T: A said today is Tuesday.

For all other versions, students will rewrite sentences you provide.

Teaching Tip:

Sentence cards are simply cards with sentences. This creates a bit of a wild card element, since everyone gets something different and is good for classes with students who tend to copy one another or for using as an early finisher activity. Don't forget to laminate them and begin with an example.

Procedure:

No materials: Prepare sentences for the students to change to reported speech. Ask one student a question, then ask another to report the answer to the class.

Other variations: Prepare cards/worksheet/PowerPoint or write on the white board 5 sentences.

If using PowerPoint or the white board, have students write their answers in their notebook.

XYZ from A to Z

Skills: Writing

Age: All

Materials Required: White board

This is a bit of a creative thinking exercise. Write the letters of the alphabet on the board, leaving enough room after each letter to fill in a word. Divide the class into groups of 3-5. Give the class a topic and have them try to fill in a word for each letter within 5 minutes. For example, Jobs: Actor, Baker, Conductor...X-ray technician, Yak farmer, Zookeeper. They might not know words such as "technician", but they may coin a term like "X-ray doctor" to get their meaning across. There probably isn't a category, even jobs or hobbies or actions, which they will be able to complete the alphabet, but students can get incredibly creative trying.

Teaching Tip:

If you want to add an element of competition (and shorten the activity), give each group a different color board marker. At the end, count the number of words in each color. In any case, definitely do not do this activity with only one board marker in use, or it will take the entire class period.

Procedure:

1. Before class, write the letters of the alphabet on the white board, leaving room after each letter to write a word.

2. Divide students into groups of 3-5 and give each group a board marker.

3. Give the class a category and 5 minutes to fill in as many words that match the category. They can only write one word per letter and should try to complete the alphabet.

4. If you gave each group a different color marker, count how many words each team contributed. The team with the most wins.

Quick Write

Skills: Writing/reading

Age: 8+

Materials Required: None, or card/white board/PowerPoint

Have students write for 5 minutes a brief response to a prompt. You can simply tell them the prompt, or display it on the white board/PowerPoint or draw a card from the Talking Bag. Here's an example of this activity: www.eslspeaking.org/quick-write.

Procedure:

1. Give students a writing prompt, either verbal or written on the white board or a PowerPoint.

2. Give them 5 minutes to write a brief response in their notebooks. Encourage them to keep writing, rather than focusing too much on grammar or spelling.

3. If you have time, you can ask a volunteer to share their response with the class.

I'm an Alien

Skills: Speaking/listening

Age: All

Materials Required: None

I love a no-prep, no-materials activity, and students generally enjoy this one. You begin class by telling the students you are an alien. You landed just a few minutes earlier, right outside the school. Since you are new here, you don't know a lot of words, and you need some help.

You can create a mission scenario, and elicit vocabulary that will help you. Maybe you want to send a letter telling your mother you arrived safely. You can elicit pen, paper, stamp, envelope, post office. Maybe you need to meet someone in another part of the school, such as the cafeteria. You can elicit types of rooms in a school (hall, bathroom, library, etc) as well as direction words.

Procedure:

1. Begin class by telling the students you are an alien. Since you are new here, you don't

know a lot of words, and you need some help.

2. Create a mission scenario, and elicit vocabulary that will help you complete it. For example, you want to send a letter telling your mother you arrived safely. You can elicit pen, paper, stamp, envelop, and post office.

3. You can give a student a chance to be the alien, if you would like to extend the activity.

Conversation Topic

Skills: Speaking/listening

Age: All

Materials Required: None

Give students a topic. They will generate questions to ask each other and have a small conversation.

Teaching Tip:

Remind students that it is more important to listen and respond to each other than to just run through their list of questions. The time given to think of several questions should simply prepare them to speak about the topic with fewer pauses.

Procedure:

1. Divide students into groups of 3-5.

2. Give them a topic from current events or popular culture, etc. and 1-2 minutes to generate 2-3 questions to ask each other.

3. Give them 5 minutes to ask and answer each other's questions.

Proof-Reading/Editing

Skills: Writing

Age: 7+

Materials Required: Worksheet/workbook/PowerPoint/white board

To keep proper usage fresh in your students' minds, they should practice frequently. This doesn't need to be a full grammar lesson; a quick warm-up can do the trick. Since this is for more advanced students, they should have a variety of errors to correct: word choice, word order, punctuation, capitalization, etc. Students should write the sentences or passage correctly.

Teaching Tip:

Begin by asking students a few review questions about whatever rules they are practicing. ("When do you use capital letters?" or "What is a run-on sentence? How can you fix it?")

Procedure:

1. In advance, prepare a worksheet or PowerPoint, or simply write several sentences on the white board. You could even take a previous workbook activity and reproduce it, if you need something quick.

2. The sentences or passage should practice previously studied points of grammar by having errors of that sort: word choice, word order, punctuation, capitalization, etc.

3. Have students correct the errors. If they are working from a PowerPoint or the white board, have them write the sentences or passage correctly in their notebooks.

Draw an Idiom

Skills: Listening/reading/speaking

Age: 10+

Materials Required: None, or white board

Give students an idiom and have them draw a picture of the idiom. Then, have them share their drawings and elicit possible meanings. Finish by giving them the actual meaning and several example sentences to write in their notebooks.

Procedure:

1. Give students an idiom, such as "raining cats and dogs" and give them 3 minutes draw a representative picture.

2. When time is up, have students share their pictures and elicit guesses about what the idiom may mean before telling students the actual meaning.

3. Finish the activity by giving students several example sentences or scenarios using the idiom for them to write in their notebooks.

Idiom Picture Prompt

Skills: Speaking

Age: 10+

Materials Required: Picture/PowerPoint

Show students a picture with a literal representation of a common idiom. Give them several minutes to discuss the possible meaning of the idiom in pairs or small groups. Finish by giving them the actual meaning and several example sentences to write in their notebooks.

Procedure:

1. In advance, prepare a PowerPoint image or picture large enough for the class to easily see.

2. Divide students into pairs or small groups and give them 3 minutes to discuss the meaning of the picture.

3. Elicit guesses about what the idiom may mean before telling students the actual meaning.

4. Finish the activity by giving students several example sentences or scenarios using the idiom for them to write in their notebooks.

Fortunately, Unfortunately / Luckily, Unluckily

Skills: Speaking/listening

Age: 9+

Materials Required: None

You may have played this game at school yourself. Start of by telling students some good news (something that "happened to you") followed by some bad news. For example, "Unfortunately, my car wouldn't start this morning. Fortunately, my neighbor gave me a ride to school. Unfortunately, she drove through a red light. Fortunately..." Students will then generate similar language using fortunately/unfortunately or luckily/unluckily.

Procedure:

1. Divide students into small groups of 3-5.

2. Give them a scenario (something that "happened to you"), alternating between good and bad news. For example, "Unfortunately, my car wouldn't start this morning. Fortunately, my neighbor gave me a ride to school. Unfortunately, she drove through a red light. Fortunately..."

3. Have students take turns within their groups adding one element at a time. Each addition should change the story from good to bad or vice versa.

4. Give students a time limit (5 minutes or so) or have them take 2-3 turns around the circle.

Word Association

Skills: Reading/writing/speaking

Age: 7+

Materials Required: Workbook or butcher paper and pens

To introduce a new topic, lesson, theme, etc., write a single relevant word in the middle of the board or paper and have students take turns adding as many words or images related to that word as possible. For large classes, have students work in groups with separate pieces of paper taped to the wall or the top of the table/ grouped desks. After a given amount of time (3-5 minutes, or when you see no one is adding anything new), discuss their answers.

Teaching Tips:

For large classes, butcher paper works best, so more students can write at one time. If that isn't possible, have 5-6 board markers available.

If using butcher paper, prepare in advance, including taping to the wall, unless students will be working at their desks. If students will be working at their desks, write the word on each table's page in advance, but don't hand them out until you have given your instructions.

Procedure:

1. Write a single word relevant to your new topic, lesson, or theme on the white board or butcher paper.
2. Have students take turns adding as many words or images related to that word as possible.
3. After 3-5 minutes (or less, if no one is adding anything new), discuss their answers.

Dictagloss

Skills: Speaking/listening

Age: 8+

Materials Required: A short story

This is a simple activity for more advanced level students that helps them practice their listening and memory skills, as well as substituting vocabulary words if the original word is no longer accessible to them. Find a short, interesting story or make up one yourself. I've used various things from children's stories to a story about something I did on the weekend. Nearly anything can work.

Tell the story 1-3 times, depending on the student level and of course you can also vary your speaking speed to make this activity easier or harder. Once you are done telling the story, students will have to go in groups of 2-3 to retell the story. Emphasize that they won't be able to recreate the exact story that you told, but that they should try their best to keep the meaning the same. Each team can join up with another team to compare. Then, tell the original story again so students can see their results. This activity works well as a writing activity too.

Teaching Tips:

It's very helpful for students to compare answers with a partner before they have to say anything in front of the class, so be sure to put them in partners or groups of three for this activity. It's helpful for the weaker students to have a stronger student getting them up to speed. It also gives students confidence that they're on the right track and they're less nervous to share their answers with the class.

Procedure:

1. Prepare a short story which you'll read to your students.

2. Put students in groups of two or three and read the story to them.

3. Students try to remember the details of the story and compare with their group. I usually only allow them to do this by speaking.

4. Read the story again and have students attempt to recreate the story more closely, again by speaking.

5. Read the story again (depending on level and difficulty of story) and the students again attempt to recreate it, even more closely.

6. Elicit a couple of teams to tell their story to the class (in a small class). Or, put two teams

together and they can tell their stories to each other (in a larger class).

7. Read the story one final time for students to compare with their own.

Describing Something Guessing Game

Skills: Speaking/listening/reading

Age: 10+

Materials Required: Handout or PowerPoint with approximately 20 pictures

This is a simple warm-up activity that you can use to generate some interest in a topic for intermediate or advanced students. It can also be used as a quick review of the last lesson's contents. For beginners, it's best to play after you've taught them the necessary language to make the sentences instead of as a warm-up at the beginning of class.

Make up a handout or PowerPoint with pictures of around 20 famous people. Give some hints, such as, "He's American," "He's a sport player," and, "He plays golf." By this time the students will have guessed Tiger Woods. You then cross Tiger Woods off their list or delete it from the PowerPoint. Turn it over to the students and they will take turns describing the people to each other.

Teaching Tips:

A sub-skill that you could focus on using this activity is hedging, which is when we are not sure about something and use language to indicate that. For example, "Maybe it's _____," "It might be _____," "Is it _____?," "It could be _____."

I emphasize that students should speak in full sentences when they are giving hints to their partners. Simply saying things like, "Man, American, golf" is really not useful for helping students improve their English skills beyond the most basic beginners and even then it's questionable. It's useful to put some example sentences on the board such as "She/He has

_____ (hair/eyes). " "She/He is from _____. " "She/He is a _____ (job). "

As a general rule, the more that you can get your students speaking in full sentences, the better off they'll be in terms of language learning. It's far easier to let your students just say one or two words, but they're not actually pushing themselves to incorporate grammar constructions into their speech in a meaningful way. Of course don't forget that spoken discourse has much shorter sentences than more formal written work, so don't push students to use more complicated grammatical constructions when doing a simple speaking activity like this.

You can put in a few fun pictures to make it more interesting. For example, I'll always include a picture of myself in a situation where it might not look like me because I had a different hairstyle or was wearing glasses. Or, I'll put in a picture of my twin sister. You can also add a picture of a student in the class or another teacher at your school that the students would know.

Procedure:
1. Prepare pictures of famous people on a handout or in a PowerPoint. PowerPoint is easier and better, but test how it will appear on the big screen first before using it in class. Sometimes low-quality pictures can look terrible when made bigger.
2. Do one example with the students so they get an idea of how to play.
3. Put the students into partners or small groups. The first student chooses someone secretly and describes him/her to his/her partner, who must guess the person, using hedging if they are unsure about the answer. You can also allow your students to ask some "W/H" questions to their partner if they wish.
4. The students switch roles and continue until the time is up.

What Am I?

Skills: Speaking/listening/reading

Age: 10+

Materials Required: Tape or pins and vocabulary words on paper

This is a classic party game that is an excellent way for beginner students to practice asking simple questions. For more advanced students, you can choose much harder vocabulary words. A good topic for advanced students (or a party you are hosting) is famous people.

Write a bunch of animals, jobs, hobbies or whatever vocabulary you want on slips of paper. Then tape or pin one to each student's back so that they can't see what it is. They have to go around to their classmates asking yes/no questions to find out what they are. For example, "Do I have four legs?" After each question, they can make a guess and the other student will answer "yes" or "no." They can only ask each student one question, so they will talk to almost everyone in the class by the end of the activity.

Teaching Tips:

Be sure to pick vocabulary that you are sure everyone is familiar with. This game really isn't fun for the student who is unlucky enough to get "armadillo."

Emphasize to students that this game is just for fun and the purpose is to enjoy themselves while practicing some questions in English. While they could just look at their own paper or get someone to tell them the word, it's not useful and it's not fun to figure out the word through cheating.

Procedure:

1. The teacher prepares slips of paper with the target vocabulary. Don't forget to laminate them if you plan on using them more than once.

2. The teacher pins or tapes one slip to each student's back.

3. Students walk around the class asking one classmate one yes/no question. The classmate answers the question and after each question, they can have one guess as to what the secret thing is.

4. If incorrect, they talk to another classmate and follow the same procedure. If correct, they take a rest, or get another paper from the teacher depending on time. A student can only ask one question to each student in the class.

Before You Go . . .

If you found lots of useful ESL warm-up activities and games, please head on over to Amazon and leave a review. It really helps this book rank more highly so that other teachers like you can find this resource. If you have any questions or we can help you in any way, please email Jackie at: wealthyenglishteacher@gmail.com or Jennifer at jenniferteacher@gmail.com. The things Jackie is most knowledgable about are: teaching in Korea, working at Korean universities, personal finance for expats, and of course teaching ESL/EFL. Jennifer is the guru of all things teaching English to children!

Made in the USA
Las Vegas, NV
24 August 2021

28708254R00028